Contents

Special pull-out chart

Sharing your Faith made easy

Mark Water

Sharing your Faith Made Easy
Hendrickson Publishers, Inc.
P.O. Box 3473
Peabody, Massachusetts 01961-3473

ISBN 1-56563-099-8

Designed and produced
by Tony Cantale Graphics

Photography supplied by Foxx Photos, Goodshoot, Digital Vision and Tony Cantale

Illustrations by
Tony Cantale Graphics

First printing — February 1999

Reprinted, 2001

Manufactured in Hong Kong

By way of introduction

1. Jesus' first *words to his disciples*

"Fishers of men"

For many Christians the whole idea of sharing one's faith is:

- a giant turn off
- a total embarrassment
- a puzzle – "How can I do it?"

When Jesus called his first disciples to follow him he gave them this promise:

> "I will make you fishers of men [and women]." *Matthew 4:19*

Conclusion No 1: Jesus says he will help us to share him with others.

2. Jesus' last *words to his disciples*

"Make disciples"

For many other Christians sharing one's faith is treated as:

- an optional extra – "I may, if I feel like it."
- a non-starter – "If Jesus wants to convert the world, he could do it without my help."

When Jesus left his eleven faithful followers he gave them this command:

> "Go and make disciples of all nations." *Matthew 28:19.*

Conclusion No 2: Jesus commands us to share our faith.

3. Why should we share our faith?

We *don't* share our faith because	We *do* share Jesus with others because
• We feel we're not up to it	• Jesus promised us his help.
• We are good/bad at it	• Jesus told us to do it.

This book will give you some handy hints on how to begin sharing your faith.

Be reasonable

Advice from an elderly fisherman

"... Always be prepared to give an answer to everyone who asks you to give the reason for the hope that you have. But do this with gentleness and respect."
1 Peter 3:15

Where to witness	Look up and read
1. Throughout the world	Mark 16:15-16
2. To strangers	John 12:20-22
3. In your home	Mark 5:19
4. In unexpected places	Acts 8:26-40
5. Among your friends	John 1:45-49

HOW TO SHARE YOUR FAITH
Hot tip No 1:
Don't argue. Do not let your discussion turn into a full scale war of words. Keep cool. Try not to lose your temper! Remember: it's possible to win the argument and lose the battle.

1 Peter 3:15

1. "Always ..."

2. "... be prepared"

3. "... to give an answer ..."

4. "... to everyone ..."

5. "... give the reason ..."

6. "... for the hope you have."

7. "... do this with gentleness and respect."

The very practical Peter

1. *Always* means always or at all times. There is no day or time of day when we are off duty as Christians.
2. *Be prepared* means make preparations to help you to share your faith. Reading through a book like this is one way to do this. Become fully familiar with the Bible.
3. *To give an answer* means that there are answers to give. You may not know all the answers now. You may never know *all* the answers. But this does not stop you from finding out some answers when you get stuck. Make use of more experienced Christians. See if one of them can help you.
4. *Everyone* means everyone (no omissions, no exceptions). You can't be too choosy who you witness to. God may give you many different kinds of people that you should witness to.
5. *Give the reason* means that the Christian faith is not anti-reason. Oh, yes, it is *faith*, but we have all been given minds by God. God commands us to love him with our *minds.* It brings no credit to Jesus if we give the impression that Christianity is irrational. If that was the case it would mean that a human mind is superior to God's mind.
6. *For the hope you have* means that we must share the hope and confidence that we have in Jesus as our Savior.
7. *Do this with gentleness and respect* means that we treat people with a kindly, understanding spirit. We don't turn people off by our attitude or demeanor.

See also: *Pray, pray, pray,* pages 38-39; *Don't ever forget the Holy Spirit,* pages 56-57.

Focus on Jesus

QUOTATION FROM A FAITHFUL SOUL WINNER TO SET YOU THINKING

"The church has nothing to do but to save souls; therefore spend and be spent in this work."
John Wesley

Jesus in the Acts of the Apostles

Jesus is the central theme throughout the Acts of the Apostles and should be our central focus.

- Peter said to the cripple who begged for money outside the temple: "Silver and gold I do not have, but what I have I give you. In the name of *Jesus Christ* of Nazareth walk." *Acts 3:6*
- To the astonished crowd who saw Peter heal this cripple, Peter said, "The God of our fathers ... has glorified his servant *Jesus*." *Acts 3:13*

The name of Jesus in the Acts of the Apostles

- In the 28 chapters of the Acts of the Apostles, *Jesus* is mentioned in over 70 verses.
- A great Bible study is to read one chapter of the Acts of the Apostles each day.
- Check out each time *Jesus* is the focus of attention for the first Christians.
- List every verse in which *Jesus* appears, with a note on the theme of the verse.
- The only chapters in which the name of *Jesus* is not seen are 12, 14, 23, 27.

Acts chapter 1	What is said about Jesus?
Verse 1	Jesus was the main theme of the gospel of Luke.
Verse 11	Jesus' ascension. Jesus will come again.
Verse 14	The virgin Mary was known as "the mother of Jesus."
Verse 16	Judas acted as a guide to those who arrested Jesus.
Verse 21	One of the qualifications for the new apostle was that he had to have known Jesus while he was on this earth.
Verse 22	Jesus' death and his resurrection.

Jesus in the Acts, even when not mentioned by name

Continuing in the Acts of the Apostles, read through one chapter at a time, and list the verses in which Jesus is referred to, but *not* mentioned by name.

The verses in chapter 1, where the name of Jesus is not mentioned, but which still have a direct reference to him are: 2, 3, 4, 5, 6, 7, 8, 9, 10, 12, 23, 24, 25.

Acts chapter 1	Where Jesus is referred to but not mentioned by name
Verse 2	Jesus' ascension
Verse 3	Jesus' death and resurrection
Verse 4	Jesus promises the coming of the Holy Spirit
Verse 5	Jesus promises that his disciples will be baptized by the Holy Spirit
Verses 6-7	Jesus answers a question from the disciples
Verse 8	Jesus tells his disciples to be his witnesses
Verses 9-10	Jesus' ascension
Verse 12	The promise that Jesus will come again
Verse 25	The apostolic ministry by Jesus' special disciples

Remember what Jesus said about himself

"I am the way and the truth and the life. No one comes to the Father except through me." *John 14:6.*

What about other religions?

It may sound almost arrogant to imply that Jesus is the only way – that there is something wrong with all other religions. But here we are dealing with a *truth* question.

This is one Bible verse that makes uncomfortable reading if one is a Jew, a Buddhist, a Hindu or a Muslim.

"Salvation is found in no one else, for there is no other name under heaven given to men by which we must be saved." Acts 4:12.

Jesus is *the* way to God. There may be many paths which lead to Christ, but Jesus is the *only* way to God.

Listen before you leap

Different approaches

Have you ever considered how many different ways Jesus spoke to people when they came to him? His approach was never the same.

Because he listened to them, he knew their specific spiritual need. What he said always met that immediate need.

Listen, listen, listen

To find out where people are spiritually, we need to pray for the Holy Spirit to help us, and to listen to what people say. Listen to their words. Observe their body language. Listen before you leap in with the gospel. Then what you say will meet their individual spiritual need.

What Jesus said to whom

In Matthew's gospel:

The person/the people	Jesus' instruction	
1. To the man with leprosy	"Be clean."	*Matthew 8:3*
2. To the believing centurion	"It will be done as you believed it would"	*Matthew 8:13*
3. To the Canaanite woman	"Your request is granted."	*Matthew 15:28*
4. To the rich young man	"Sell your possessions and give to the poor."	*Matthew 19:21*

In John's gospel:

The person/the people	Jesus' instruction	
1. To Philip	"Follow me."	*John 1:43*
2. To Nicodemus	"You must be born again."	*John 3:7*
3. To the Samaritan woman who wanted water	"I give ... a spring of water welling up to eternal life."	*John 4:14*
4. To the man who had not walked for thirty-eight years	"Get up! ... and walk."	*John 5:8*
5. To the man born blind	"I am the light of the world."	*John 9:5*
6. To Jews asking, "Are you the Christ?"	"I give eternal life."	*John 10:28*
7. To Martha in her bereavement	"I am the resurrection and the life"	*John 11:25*

What is the best book on how can I share Jesus?

The best book to learn more about witnessing for Jesus is the New Testament. Go through Mark's and Luke's Gospel and make similar tables to the one above.

- Note the variety of people Jesus spoke to.
- Note how what Jesus said fit exactly what that person needed to hear.

The ABCD of sharing your faith

"He who wins souls is wise." *Proverbs 11:30*
So, how does one go about "winning souls": that is, introducing people to Jesus?

There are countless ways. Here is one very simple way. If you find it helpful, you can make use of it. If you don't find it helpful, you can try some other way. It's not meant to be a slick technique. It is simply a straightforward way of helping someone who wants to know how to make the Lord Jesus Christ to become their friend and Savior.

ABCD

This is just a useful way for you to remember four things, as you attempt to lead a person to Jesus. You go through four things, from A to D.

A stands for *Admit*
B stands for *Believe*
C stands for *Come to Jesus*
D stands for *Details*

The next eight pages go through each of these.

What do I actually say?

Over the next eight pages there are sections to suggest what you actually say, as you go through the ABCD of the plan of salvation. Now you don't have to use these words; you can say the same thing using your own words.

- The *What do I actually say?* sections are put there to make it crystal clear what point you are trying to cover at each stage.
- In the same way the *What do I actually pray?* section is only a guide. You can use totally different words and still be praying for the same thing.
- Also, in the *What do I actually write?* section, the letter is only a guide and you can make up your own to cover the same things.

The *What do I actually ...?* sections are intended to be examples for people who want help, step-by-step.

It's a friendship with a friend

- Being a Christian is being a friend with Jesus.
- Becoming a Christian is starting this friendship.

Don't be confused by the many different ways in which this friendship is described in the Bible and by Christians today. Sometimes you read about or hear the following phrases – don't worry, they all mean the same thing.

"Coming to Christ"

"Turning to Jesus"

"Putting one's faith in Jesus"

"Accepting Christ"

"Becoming a Christian"

"Inviting Jesus into my life"

"Being converted"

"Being born again"

"Being born from above"

"Being born by the Spirit"

"I was forgiven by Jesus"

"I came to know Jesus as my friend"

"Committing yourself to Jesus"

"I started to follow Christ"

"You are a new person in Jesus"

Try not to confuse the person you are sharing your faith with. The best thing to do is to follow one way of speaking about "becoming a Christian." Try to stick to that one way.

One of the most helpful ways to do this is to talk about Jesus being a friend.

A is for Admit

The spiritual condition of those who do not know Jesus

Their spiritual state	Look up and read
1. They are in a state of death	*Romans 6:23*
2. They are perishing	*1 Corinthians 1:18*
3. They have no hope	*Ephesians 2:12*
4. They are condemned by God	*John 3:18*
5. They are spiritually dead	*Ephesians 2:1*
6. They are under God's wrath	*John 3:36*
7. They have neither God nor Jesus	*Ephesians 2:12*

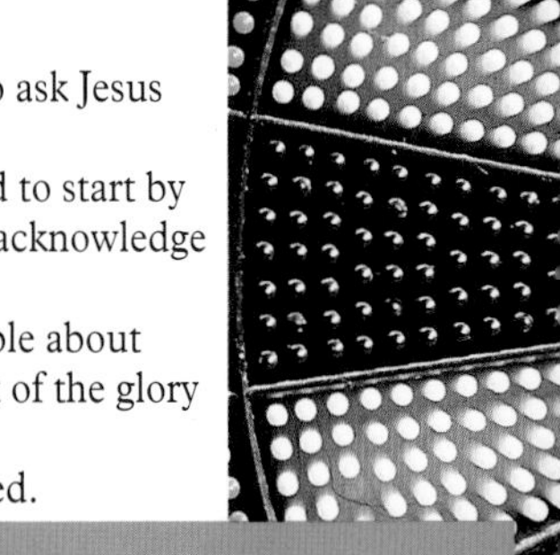

It's not necessary that the person you are trying to introduce to Jesus knows all this! You're just trying to help them to get started. But it is helpful for you to realize what the Bible teaches about everyone being a sinner in God's eyes.

What do I actually say?

"It's so wonderful that you want to ask Jesus to be your Friend.

The Bible explains that we need to start by admitting something. We need to acknowledge that we are sinful in God's sight.

Here's a helpful verse in the Bible about this. 'All have sinned and fall short of the glory of God.' *Romans 3:23*

Everyone in the world has sinned.

God is perfect and we are far from being perfect. This is what the Bible calls sin.

To sin: is to violate God's law, to miss the mark of perfection or to step outside the boundary of right into wrong.

The first thing you have to do in order to have Jesus as your friend is to admit that you are a sinner."

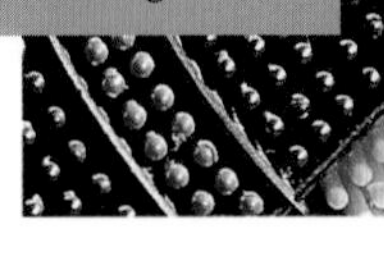

Don't *worry if ...*

- You get tongue-tied.
- You find that you are embarrassed. Do your best to focus on the person you are trying to help and to forget about yourself.
- You drop your Bible, forget a Bible verse or lose your way. Remember A, B, C, D and then cover each point as best as you can.

Do *worry if ...*

- You think this is too easy for words and it is something you will just sail through.
- You don't pray before you start and after you have finished.
- You are not humbled that God should use you to introduce someone to Jesus
- You ever lose the wonder of this.

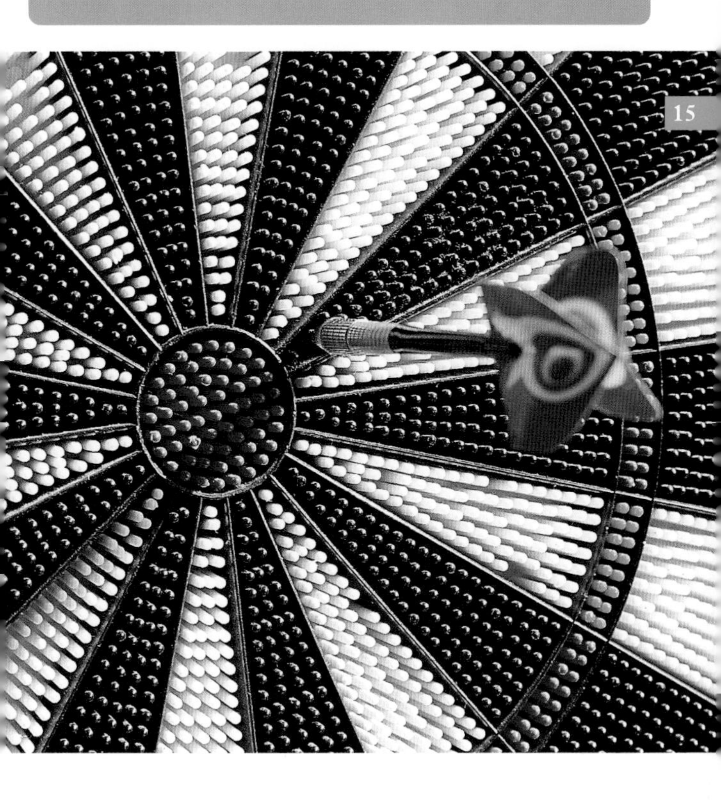

B is for Believe

Some handy hints

1. Use your Bible

- If you're sitting down with a person, get out your Bible and read a verse from the Bible to explain what you are saying.
- If you're walking along a street and talking, make sure that you somehow get across the point that what you are saying is not your own clever idea but that it comes from the Bible – that it is God's idea.

2. Don't confuse

- If you are reading verses from your Bible, don't look up dozens and dozens – that is likely to confuse the person you are trying to help. Just hone in on one or a few.

3. Keep it short

- Don't take all night. Don't preach a sermon. Don't try and cover every angle. Be brief. Just explain each point of the A, B, C, D as simply as you can.

What do I actually say?

"To have Jesus as your Friend, the Bible says that you need to believe that he can help you.

Since we are all sinners in God's sight, Jesus came into our world to help us.

Jesus came to deal with our sin problem. This verse offers help to understand this. It tells us why Jesus died on the cross. 'He himself [that is, Jesus] bore our sins in his own body on the tree [that is, the cross].' *1 Peter 2:24*

The apostle Peter says that Jesus took our sins on himself when he died on the cross. Let me illustrate this:

1. Here I am *(put out your left hand)*
2. Because, like everyone, I am a sinner, it's as if I'm weighed down and burdened by sin *(put a large object such as a book, wallet, car keys on a clean handkerchief into the palm of your left hand. This object is to represent sin)*.
3. When Jesus died on the cross for us, he took our sin on himself. *(Turn your left hand over into the palm of your right hand so that the object used is now in your right hand. Hold out your empty left hand. The object is now gone. Then hold out your right hand with the object sitting in your palm.)*

4. Now *(move your left hand up and down two or three times)* our sin (and the weight of our sin) has been taken away from us.
5. This verse is saying that it's easy to see where our sin is. It's been placed on Jesus *(move your right hand – with the object in the palm of your hand – up and down two or three times.)*

The second thing you have to do for Jesus to be your friend is to believe that Jesus died for you."

Some more handy hints

- You don't have to repeat the Bible references to the person you are speaking to.
- Memorize the Bible verses you use.
- Write down the verses on the inside back cover of your Bible. Then you won't worry in case you forget them (if you have memorized them) or that you may remember them incorrectly. Here's how to write them down.

A stands for	Admit that I am a sinner	Romans 3:23	Page number ... *(of your Bible)*
B stands for	Believe that Jesus died for me	1 Peter 2:24	Page number ...
C stands for	Come to Jesus	Revelation 3:20	Page number ...

See also: *The Bridge*, pages 40-41

C is for Come to Jesus

What do I actually say?

"Once you are ready to admit that you are a sinner ... once you believe that Jesus took your sin on him when he died for you ... it is time for action. The third thing necessary to have Jesus as your friend – is to do something.

The Bible explains how we start our friendship with Jesus in this verse. 'Here I am! I stand at the door and knock. If anyone hears my voice and opens the door, I will come in and eat with him, and he with me.' *Revelation 3:20*

This verse pictures Jesus standing outside a door. The idea is that he is trying to get into a house and he is knocking at the door.

The door represents our lives. Jesus knocks on the door of our lives and he wants us to open the door and say, 'Come in. Please come in Lord Jesus.'

Until now Jesus has been, as it were, outside your life. Having Jesus as your friend means asking him to step inside (into) your life.

So the third thing you have to do in order to have Jesus as your friend is to come to Jesus and invite him into your life."

A prayer asking Jesus into a person's life

"Would you like to invite Jesus into your life now and have him as your friend? *(If the answer is 'yes,' or a nod of the head, continue.)*

Would you like me to lead you in a personal prayer that you make your own – asking Jesus into your life? *(If the answer is 'yes,' or a nod of the head, continue.)*"

What do I actually pray?

"Here is a prayer you can pray line by line after me. You can pray it audibly or silently.

'Lord Jesus Christ *(pause for a second or two at the end of each line to allow time for the person you are helping to pray the prayer)*, I know that I have sinned and am sorry for my sins. *(Pause)*

Thank you for dying on the cross to take away my sin. *(Pause)*

I want you to be my special friend. *(Pause)*

Please come into my life now. *(Pause)*

I want you as my Savior and friend for ever. *(Pause)*

Amen. *(Pause)*"

A prayer for you to pray

If the person has prayed the above prayer, pray a prayer along the following lines. This is a prayer you are praying and is not like the above prayer which is a prayer for the other person to pray.

"Lord Jesus Christ thank you for coming into ____'s *(say the person's name here, and in the following blanks)* life.

Please help ____ to become a closer and closer friend with you throughout his/her life.

Please help ____ to find help from other Christians.

Please help ____ to serve you all his/her life, with the help of the Holy Spirit. Amen."

D is for details

1. Because baptism is the initial reaction to accepting Christ in the New Testament – be certain the person gives attention to this need to be baptized

Throughout the New Testament a person's initial reaction to accepting Jesus as their Savior was to submit to baptism. Baptism depicts two things. First, it depicts as an object lesson the death, the burial and the resurrection of Jesus. Secondly, it portrays for the Christian the death to sin, the burial of the old life and the resurrection to a new life. For further study on this topic, see *Matthew 3:13-17; Acts 2:37-39; 8:26-40; 16:25-34; and Romans 6:3-7.*

2. Make sure the person is linked up to a helpful Christian fellowship

Determine whether the person already goes to a church where he/she will find spiritual help. If not, ask if you can take his/her name and address/phone number. You need to get the person's permission for you to aid them in finding a church that will help provide spiritual growth. Then provide the individual with the details.

3. Encourage the person to read the Bible every day

It is very important for the person to read the Bible for him/herself and to pray each day. Make certain that the person has a Bible, some Bible helps or tools and then provide some instructions.

If you don't have any Bible helps to pass on say, "Try reading one chapter from Mark's Gospel each day. And then move on and do the same with Matthew, Luke and John."

4. Write a letter

If the individual lives far away, a personal letter from you is likely to be appreciated.

Points to cover

1. "How wonderful that you have asked Jesus to be your Friend." Without preaching a sermon you need to cover the following points, especially if the person is not linked up to a Christian fellowship.

2. "The friendship you have just started is the beginning of a new life with Jesus.

There are a number of things helpful in a friendship with Jesus:

a. Keep on deepening your friendship with Jesus. Pray to him daily plus make Bible reading a part of each day. These activities will help to make Jesus more real.

b. Tell other people about Jesus, even though this can be difficult at times. How you live is as important in witnessing as what you say.

c. Join with other Christians in worship and in informal times of praising God. It is also helpful to get involved in a weekly Bible study."

3. If you have details about a helpful church, provide them.

4. Close by saying that you will be praying for him/her. If you intend to pray for him/her every day, you should tell them so.

More follow-up

Paul's aim

Paul never said that it was his aim to win as many people as possible for Jesus. Paul did say, "We proclaim [Jesus] ... so that we may present everyone perfect in Christ." *Colossians 1:28.*

It's hard to overemphasize the importance of follow-up.

Follow-up means making sure that a new Christian has the means to survive and grow.

Wesley and Whitefield

John Wesley and George Whitefield were both greatly used by God as they preached in America and through the length and breadth of England.

At the end of his life Whitefield admitted that he wished he had been like Wesley in his follow-up methods. Wesley tried to make sure that all the people who became Christians through his preaching joined in a local, weekly meeting with other Christians, so they could pray, study the Bible together, and offer one another guidance and encouragement.

Whitefield wrote in his Journal

"My brother Wesley acted more wisely than I. The souls that were awakened under his ministry he joined together in classes, and so preserved the fruit of his labors. I failed to do this, and as a result my people are a rope of sand."

Wesley wrote in his Journal

"I determined by the grace of God not to strike one blow in any place where I cannot follow the blow."

Follow up is part of leading someone to Jesus

Don't think that your work is over once you've helped someone to accept Christ as Savior. Your work may have only just started.

Your responsibility is to make sure that they have the means to be linked up to a Christian fellowship.

When people become Christians they are said to be spiritual babies. They are like "newborn babies" according to Peter, s*ee 1 Peter 2:2.*

Human babies take many years before they can stand on their own feet and fend for themselves. Follow up work may take many years.

What you can do

Your job is not to make them grow spiritually, only the Holy Spirit does that. Your job is to encourage and guide.

Sometimes all you will have to do is to pass along their name to another Christian or church leader who will take on this responsibility. Sometimes you will be able to do some or all of the following things:

1. Pray daily for the person.

2. Write a follow up letter.

3. Ensure that the person has information about a local helpful Christian group.

What are the marks of a good church? Look for a church where:

a. Jesus Christ is at the center of the worship and all activities

b. The Bible is preached and taken seriously

4. Provide helpful introductory Bible reading suggestions.

5. Pass along a booklet that explains how one becomes a Christian. It is especially important to choose one which explains about assurance (being sure that one is a Christian). If there is no confidence and security as a Christian, then, as Jesus said, "The evil one comes and snatches what was sown in his heart." *Matthew 13:19.* If you think that a person won't read such a booklet you may have to write a letter, simply explaining what assurance and security in Christ means. See pages 24-25.

Using the Bible

The Bible is your authority

Your own ultimate authority in matters about the Christian faith is the Bible. So when you share your faith, you should not continually say, "I think this, I think that." The person you are talking needs to know that your ideas are based on what the Bible says. So, instead of saying, "What I think about sin is ..."; you may say, "What the Bible teaches about sin is ..."

Some people like to ask the person they are trying to lead to Jesus to read out aloud the Bible verses they are referring to. This may help to make the point that your authority comes from the Bible. (However, this may be too much of an ordeal for some people who may not be too familiar with the Bible and it could turn out to be embarrassing for them.)

Remember: all Scripture is inspired by God

"All Scripture is God-breathed and is useful for teaching, rebuking, correcting and training in righteousness, so that the man of God may be thoroughly equipped for every good work." *2 Timothy 3:16*

Being sure that Jesus is your friend

Here's a draft paragraph about Christian assurance you could include in a follow up letter. You will see that it takes a Bible verse as the basis for what it says.

What do I actually write?

Many new Christians have doubts and wonder if Jesus really did become their friend. If that happens to you, you may like to know that this is quite normal! Here is a plan of action to counter such doubts.

1. Read the verse from Revelation chapter three, verse twenty, in your own Bible.
"Here I am! I stand at the door and knock. If anyone hears my voice and opens the door, I will come in and eat with him, and he with me."

2. Ask yourself: "Did I sincerely ask Jesus to come into my life?"

3. Note carefully the promise Jesus makes in this verse. What does he say if someone does open the door to him?

4. Jesus' promise is: "I will come in."

He does *not* say, "I may come in."

He does *not* say, "I will come in but will leave you if you sin."

5. Jesus has promised to enter the door of your life if you invite him in. As a result you can rest assured that he has come into your life and that he is your Friend. We need to remember that Jesus is the Son of God and we are putting our trust in him and his promises and not in ourselves and our doubts.

Another good passage on Christian assurance: 1 John 5:11-13

Verse 11: And this is the testimony: God has given us eternal life, and this life is in his Son.

Verse 12: He who has the Son has life; he who does not have the Son of God does not have life.

Verse 13: I write these things to you who believe in the name of the Son of God so that you may know that you have eternal life.

These verses teach:

a. that God wants us to *know* that we have eternal life, that is life with Jesus for ever;

b. that eternal life is God's gift to us;

c. that we have eternal life as we have believed in Jesus.

The power of the written word

Have a Bible study

- Have a Bible study with an unconverted friend. Many people think only of having Bible studies with other Christians. But for a person who really wants to learn about Jesus Christ, there is no better way to help him/her than to have a Bible study together.
- Have a Bible study with a brand new Christian.

What should we study?

- For a non-Christian try John 3:1-16, and for a second Bible study, John 4:1-54.
- For a new Christian you could go through the theme of the way of salvation. Here are some headings with the relevant Bible verses to look up and discuss.

The way of salvation

A is for Admit: Admitting that we are sinners and need Jesus: *Romans 3:23; Romans 6:23; Isaiah 59:2*

B is for Belief: Believing in Jesus and his death for us: *Isaiah 53:5-6; 1 Peter 3:18; 1 Peter 2:24*

C is for Coming to Jesus: *Revelation 3:20; John 1:12; Acts 8:26-40*

Verses on Christian assurance: *1 John 5:11-13; John 6:37*

Letter of dedication

Some people have found it very reassuring to have a written record about the moment they asked Jesus to be their Friend. You could suggest the following as suitable wording for a new Christian to write out and keep.

Lord Jesus,
I admit that I am a sinner.
I want to turn from my sin.
I believe that you died for my sin.
Please come into my life
to be my Friend and Savior.
Amen.

Signature ....

Date ....

The ministry of Christian literature

- Find some up-to-date booklets that explain how to begin living the Christian life.
- Other useful booklets for new Christians are:

a. Daily Devotionals and Read through the Bible guides. These are available for different age groups and different levels of Christian understanding.
b. Evangelistic tracts. These often contain true conversion stories.

One short visit to a Christian Bookstore would help you stock up with many of these witnessing/sharing resources.

Some Christians set aside money each month to buy Christian books and booklets for other people.

See also: *Using the Internet*, page 64

A link in the chain

Paul's conversion

We often think that the most famous conversion of all time came out of the blue and that Jesus spoke directly to Paul without any human being involved.

A flash of light from heaven

Read through Paul's conversion in **Acts 9:1-20** and see how wonderfully Paul met with the risen Lord Jesus.

v.1-2 Some people are converted when they least expect it.

v.3-4 Nobody is beyond being converted by God. Many of the worst persecutors of Christians have themselves become converted.

v.5 It became clear to Saul that he was having an encounter with Jesus.

v.6 Saul had to be told. He did not himself know what to do.

v.7 Other people are often mystified by the Christian conversion process.

v.10 Ananias was alert to God. Have you ever thought how important Ananias was in Paul's conversion?

v.11 Humanly speaking, Paul would have been nowhere without Ananias.

v.12 When God wants you to speak to someone, he will prepare the person.

v.13-15 Sometimes we have to expect the unexpected. Even Ananias got some things wrong but because he was obedient God overruled.

v.16 Living the Christian life involves difficulties. It's not all easy sailing.

v.17 All true conversions center on Jesus and the Holy Spirit.

v.18 Baptism was a sign and culmination of conversion.

v.19 Fellowship with other Christians is vital for new Christians.

v.20 Few new Christians openly witness about Jesus more quickly than Paul did!

Giving your testimony

When a Christian tells a group of people how he/she became a Christian it is sometimes called giving one's testimony.

The idea is that the Christian should be sharing about God's grace and about the way he/she came to commit his/her life to

Jesus. If you are ever asked to do this, there are two pitfalls to be aware of:

- Don't imply that it was more spectacular than it really was;
- And point to Jesus and not to yourself.

John the Baptist got it exactly right when he said, speaking of Jesus, "He must become greater; I must become less." *John 3:30*

Paul never tired of giving his testimony. Luke records it three times. *See Acts 9:1-19; Acts 22:4-16; 26:9-18*

A link in the chain

You could say that there were a number of hidden factors behind Paul's conversion.

We do not know just how much of an impression Stephen's martyrdom had on Paul.

Clearly Luke thought it was significant as he says that the people who stoned Stephen to death, "laid their clothes at the feet of a young man named Saul." *Acts 7:58*

Luke concludes Stephen's martyrdom by saying, "And Saul was there, giving approval to his death." *Acts 8:1*

When you seek to share your faith remember that you are one link in a chain.

- You may be the first link, setting someone thinking about God in general.
- You may be a middle link, helping someone to see clearly who Jesus is.
- You may be the last link, showing someone how they can ask Jesus into their lives.

Planting and watering

Paul angrily scolded the Christians at Corinth for splitting themselves into divisive groups and then following particular Christian leaders.

Paul's answer to all this was to say, "I planted the seed, Apollos watered it, but God made it grow." *1 Corinthians 3:6*

So it does not matter which link in the chain you are. The important thing is for us to do our part faithfully and to remember that God is the one who carries out his work in people's lives. "God makes his seed grow."

I've never done this before

QUOTATION FROM A FAITHFUL SOUL WINNER TO SET YOU THINKING

"Even if I were utterly selfish and had no care for anything but my own happiness I would choose, if I might, under God, to be a soul-winner; for never did I know perfect overflowing, unutterable happiness of the purest and most ennobling order till I first heard of one who had sought and found the Savior through my means.

"No young mother ever so rejoiced over her first born child, no warrior was so exultant over a hard won victory." *C.H. Spurgeon*

Know-how or courage?

For most people lack of courage, rather than lack of know-how, stops them from sharing their faith.

There are ways to build up your courage.

Building block one – overcoming the fear of rejection

Jesus said that we should expect to be persecuted. "They persecuted me, they will persecute you." *John 15:20.*

Now, nobody likes to be rejected or laughed at, or thought to be a religious fanatic. Someone has said that it is easier to face guns than to face grins.

a. Pray and ask others to pray for you

We have to ask God for courage to overcome our fear of being rejected or we'll never start. Paul was only too aware of his own fears in sharing the gospel. He asked other Christians to pray for him about such matters. We should do exactly the same. Paul wrote, "Pray also for me, that whenever I open my mouth, words may be given me so that I will fearlessly make known the mystery of the gospel." *Ephesians 6:19.*

b. Be a fool for Jesus

Be prepared to be a fool for Jesus, especially when you are made fun of. Paul wrote, "We are fools for Christ." *1 Corinthians 4:10.*

c. Please God not people

Sort out in your mind who you are trying to please. Are you trying to keep up appearances before people, or are you trying to serve God? Peter was hauled before the top Jewish Council, the Sanhedrin, accused (as if it was a crime) of peaching about Jesus. Peter's bold reply was: "We must obey God rather than men!" *Acts 5:29.*

Building block two – Do something you *can* manage

If you find the idea of witnessing to total strangers too much to cope with, do something that you can manage.

You may find it easier to write to, or e-mail somebody about Jesus rather than talking to them face to face or phoning them.

Possibly it may be easier to give an evangelistic booklet than explain the way of salvation yourself. If this is so, carry around with you some tracts, so you can give them away at the appropriate time. Some people even enclose tracts when paying their bills! You may be able to lend a Christian video or Christian book to a friend.

Develop a positive rather than a negative attitude. Don't say, "I can't preach in public. I can't witness to strangers. I don't think I'll do anything!" Do what you can do. Don't worry about what you can't do.

HOW TO SHARE YOUR FAITH
Hot tip No 2:
Start your own note book. Every time you learn something that is going to help you share your faith, write it down in your notebook. As a reminder of the lesson you learned, put a date beside it. This will help you reflect back on what you learned on that day.

Go for variety

Paul as a model soul-winner

Why did Paul witness to Jesus?	Look up and read	More verses to look up and read
1. Because he was commanded to:	*Romans 10:9-10*	*Matthew 10:32-33; Psalm 107:2*
2. Because he was not ashamed to:	*Romans 1:16*	
3. Because of what Jesus had done for him:	*Romans 5:1-2*	*Psalm 40:1-3*

All things to all people

Paul was often misunderstood – even by fellow Christians!

He cared more about helping people spiritually than about what other Christians might say.

He explained this when the wrote to the Christians at Corinth: "I have become all things to all men so that by all possible means I might save some." *1 Corinthians 9:22*

Paul's example	What does that mean for you?
"I have become all things ...	Certainly this would include showing a genuine interest in what other people are interested in – obviously, excluding things that are clearly evil!
... to all men ...	All men means all people – men and women. Paul knew how to appeal to top Jewish leaders, as well as to those who had no interest, whatsoever, in Christianity. This means that we should be happy to share our faith with all kinds of different people, without thinking about their background, age, class, race, profession or social standing.
... so that by all possible means ...	Paul used every available God-given means to spread the gospel. Today Christians have access to various forms of media that can be used for sharing their faith – the radio, TV, videos, the Internet, attractive Christians books, CD's and cassettes, and even computer software. (How about watching a Christian video with a friend who may not be ready to go to church with you?)
... I might save some."	Paul never lost sight of his goal – to be a means of introducing people to Jesus, the Savior.

HOW TO SHARE YOUR FAITH
Hot tip No 3:
Conversion has been defined as: "Committing all I know of me to all I know of Christ." As you share your faith, point the person you are talking to, to Jesus.

What does "born again" mean?

Nicodemus goes to Jesus

The phrase comes from the conversation Nicodemus had with Jesus. *See John 3:1-16.*

Jesus said to him, "You must be born again." *John 3:7.*

It is one way of describing how one becomes a Christian. Books of theology sometimes call this the doctrine of regeneration. ("To bring new life and energy to that which is dead.")

What this new birth is not

• The new birth is not being highly religious.

If anyone could have reached heaven by living a religious life and doing good deeds it was Nicodemus. According to John 3:1 he was a Pharisee.

• The new birth is not doing lots of good deeds.

"For it is by grace you have been saved, through faith – and this not from yourselves, it is the gift of God – not by works, so that no one can boast." *Ephesians 2:8-9. See also Matthew 7:21-23*

Portrait of Nicodemus the Pharisee

- He fasted twice a week.
- He gave away 10% of his income.
- Every day he prayed for two hours in the synagogue.
- He had learned the first five books of the Bible – word for word.

But it was to this important Pharisee that Jesus said, "You must be born again." And Jesus told him this three times – in case he did not get the message the first time, which he did not! *See John 3:3, 5, 7*

Some Bible definitions of new birth

- **A divine birth**
  "No one who is born of God will continue to sin, because God's seed remains in him; he cannot go on sinning, because he has been born of God." *1 John 3:9*
- **A new creation**
  "Therefore, if anyone is in Christ, he is a new creation; the old has gone, the new has come!" *2 Corinthians 5:17*
- **A spiritual awakening**
  "He saved us, not because of righteous things we had done, but because of his mercy. He saved us through the washing of rebirth and renewal by the Holy Spirit." *Titus 3:5*

The need, the way, and the result of a new birth

The need for a new birth

1. It is universal. Everyone needs it. *Jeremiah 17:9-10; Titus 3:3; Romans 3:23*
2. We cannot change ourselves. *Jeremiah 13:23; Ephesians 2:8-9*
3. Jesus said we must be born again. *John 3:3, 5, 7*
4. The new birth is essential because of God's holiness. *Hebrews 12:14*

The way to a new birth

1. By hearing and believing the gospel. *James 1:18; Romans 10:17*
2. It is God's work carried out by the Holy Spirit. *Titus 3:5; John 16:7-9*
3. By a personal decision to believe who Jesus is and trust him to do what he has promised. *Acts 16:31-33; John 1:12; Titus 3:5*

The result of a new birth

1. Becoming a child of God. *John 1:12-13*
2. The forgiveness of sin. *Acts 2:38-39*
3. The living presence of the Holy Spirit. *1 Corinthians 3:16-17*
4. Living a righteous life. *Titus 2:14; 1 John 2:29*
5. A love for fellow Christians. *1 John 3:14*

Dealing with diversions and smoke screens

Jesus speaks with the woman from Samaria

There is perhaps no better example in the New Testament of how to do personal evangelism, than the story of Jesus speaking with the woman from Samaria.

Work your way through John 4:1-42 and see how many lessons you can learn from seeing Jesus the master winner of souls at work.

A summary of John 4:1-42

Verses	What Jesus did
1-7	Jesus made contact
8-15	Jesus aroused her spiritual interest
16-18	Jesus did not ignore her sin
19-24	*J*esus dealt with her diversionary tactic
25-26	Jesus challenged her to commit herself to him

How Jesus dealt with a red herring

"Sir," the woman said, "I can see that you are a prophet. Our fathers worshiped on this mountain, but you Jews claim that the place where we must worship is in Jerusalem."

Jesus declared, "Believe me, woman, a time is coming when you will worship the Father neither on this mountain nor in Jerusalem. You Samaritans worship what you do not know; we worship what we do know, for salvation is from the Jews. Yet a time is coming and has now come when the true worshipers will worship the Father in spirit and truth, for they are the kind of worshipers the Father seeks. God is spirit, and his worshipers must worship in spirit and in truth."
Verses 19-24

What the woman tried to do
Jesus' probing question was getting too close for comfort. She tried to steer the conversation away from herself, her sinful life and her spiritual need of God. She was looking for a less personal question.

How Jesus refused to be diverted
Jesus did answer her question, but immediately redirected the conversation back into a spiritual direction. He said, "God is spirit, and his worshipers must worship in spirit and truth."

Dealing with diversions

- Distinguish between a diversion and a genuine question.
- Remember: you don't have to answer a person's diversionary tactic the moment it is raised. You could say, "That's a very interesting question. Would you mind if we left it on one side for the time being?" And then return to the spiritual issue you are talking about.
- When God is convicting a person they usually try every way possible to escape. So don't be surprised by smoke screens, but don't let them divert you from the main purpose of your conversation.

Frequently raised diversions and smoke screens

What kind of answer could you give to these questions and difficulties if they were raised as you were trying to lead a person to Jesus? (Don't be a know-it-all.) Admit to doubts and difficulties when you have them.

1. What about other religions?
2. Did God create the world in seven days?
3. I have a different idea about God than you have.
4. I don't believe in the existence of God.
5. I don't believe that the Bible is the word of God.
6. How can you place such trust in the Bible? Isn't it full of contradictions?
7. I don't believe that Jesus was the Son of God.
8. What about all the suffering in the world?

12 lessons on soul winning from John 4

The lesson	Other verses
1. Make the most of any opportunity. *v.7*	*Colossians 4:5*
2. Establish contact through asking a question. *v.7*	*Luke 18:40*
3. Don't be aggressive. Be ready to admit your own need. *v.7*	*James 3:17-18*
4. Don't be put off by a lack of spiritual understanding. *v.10*	*1 Corinthians 2:14*
5. Talk about God and his gift of salvation. *v.10*	*Romans 6:23*
6. Draw spiritual truths from everyday things. *vv.10-12*	*Matthew 6:26-28*
7. Keep the conversation on spiritual matters. *v.13*	*John 3:3*
8. Show how appealing and satisfying Jesus is. *vv.13-14*	*Psalm 107:9; Acts 10:38*
9. Confront the sinner with the fact that he/she is a sinner. *v.16*	*Romans 3:23*
10. Watch out for diversions and smoke screens. *vv.19-21*	*Mark 9:33-37*
11. Do not be vague and fuzzy. *v.25*	*John 11:25*
12. God reveals himself through Jesus and his word. *v.26*	*Matthew 16:16-17*

Pray, pray, pray

The priority of prayer

Prayer is an important element in sharing your faith.

How to pray for yourself

- Pray that you may be close to Jesus.
- Pray that you will be used by Jesus.
- Pray when you are at the point of sharing your faith. Pray as you are about to speak. Pray as you knock on a door.

How to pray for non-Christians

- That the Holy Spirit will prepare their hearts.
- That the Holy Spirit will remove the veil from their hearts.

See 2 Corinthians 3:12-16.

Don't forget that you're fighting a spiritual war

The devil will do everything he can to stop you from witnessing for Jesus.

Paul often spoke about Christians being caught up in a spiritual fight. He said,

"our struggle is not against flesh and blood,
but against the rulers,
against the authorities,
against the powers of this dark world
and against the spiritual forces of evil
in the heavenly realms."

That's why he told them: "Therefore put on the full armor of God."

(See Ephesians 6:11-12).

Pray for those you have lead to the Lord

Anyone who has been helped by you to accept Christ has a very special spiritual link with you. So you have a responsibility to pray for them.

The apostle Paul called himself a father to those he had led to Christ, and he called the people he led to Christ his sons (children).

1. Timothy

"To Timothy my true *son* in the faith."	*1 Timothy 1:2*
"My *son,* I give you this instruction."	*1 Timothy 1:18*
"To Timothy, my dear *son.*"	*2 Timothy 1:2*
"My *son,* be strong in the grace that is in Christ Jesus."	*2 Timothy 2:1*

2. Christians at Corinth

"Even though you have ten thousand guardians in Christ, you do not have many fathers, for in Christ Jesus I became your *father* in the gospel."	*1 Corinthians 4:15*

3. Onesimus (a converted runaway slave)

"I appeal to you for my *son* Onesimus, who became my *son* while I was in chains."	*Philemon 10*

4. Titus

"To Titus, my true *son* in our common faith."	*Titus 1:4*

See also: *Don't ever forget the Holy Spirit*, pages 56-57.

The bridge

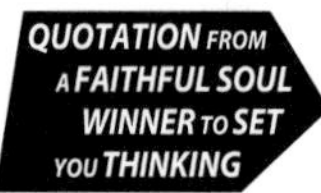

"I look upon this world as a wrecked vessel. God has given me a lifeboat and said to me: 'Moody, save all you can.'" *D.L. Moody.*

The bridge to God

There are many different illustrations you can use as you share Jesus. One helpful idea is the concept of a bridge.

A good question to ask someone who entertains doubts about Jesus and about why he died on the cross is as follows:

Question: "If you could climb to heaven under your own power, why then would God allow Jesus to suffer and sacrifice his life?"

Answer: "God sent Jesus as a bridge between us and God. The bridge was in the shape of a cross spanning the gap between earth and heaven."

Four steps

There are four steps for a non-Christian to take in order to cross over this bridge to God. The four steps are four ideas or truths he/she needs to accept.

Step 1: to cross the bridge
God loves us and has a great plan for our lives.

- Read together a verse about God's love. *John 3:16.*

Step 2: to cross the bridge
Our sin separates us from God so we can't experience God's plan and love for us. Our sin makes a tremendously wide gap, as it were, between us and God.

- Read together a verse about God's love. *Romans 3:23; 6:23.*

Step 3: to cross the bridge
God sent Jesus to bridge the gap between us and God. Jesus did this when he died on the cross for our sins.

- Read together a verse about God's love. *Romans 5:8*

Step 4: to cross the bridge
Step four is to actually cross over the bridge. We do this by allowing Jesus into our lives as our friend and Savior.

- Read together a verse about God's love. *John 1:12; 3:3-5; Titus 3:5.*

Informal missionaries

Adolf Harnack, in his massive book, *The Mission and Expansion of Christianity*, wrote: "We cannot hesitate to believe that the great mission of Christianity was accomplished by means of informal missionaries."

All Christians are "informal" missionaries in this sense.

Time to get tough

John the Baptist and the blunt approach

John the Baptist believed in the direct approach to personal evangelism. Wherever he went he seemed to shoot from the hip! Some people seem to have the gift of being able to boldly engage people and then speak about Jesus. You may not be able to do this, but you can pray for those who can.

John's message: "Repent."

• To crowds of ordinary people

John's message to them was: "Repent, for the kingdom of heaven is near." *Matthew 3:1*
The result: They confessed their sins, "and were baptized by him [John] in the Jordan River." *Matthew 3:6*

• To top religious leaders

John called the Pharisees and Sadducees, "You brood of vipers!" *Matthew 3:7*
John's message to them was: "Produce fruit in keeping with repentance. And do not think that you can say to yourselves, 'We have Abraham as our father.'" *Matthew 3:9*

Peter's message: "Repent."

• To those who had crucified Christ

Peter's message to those who recognized their sinfulness and "were cut to the heart" was, "Repent and be baptized, every one of you ..." *Acts 2:38*
The result: "Those who accepted his message were baptized, and about three thousand were added to their number that day." *Acts 2:41*

Key verse about John the Baptist's witness to Jesus

John the Baptist said, "He [Jesus] must become greater, I must decrease." *John :3:30*

See also: *Softly, softly*, pages 44-45; *The importance of preaching*, pages 60-61.

Five ways not to share your faith

1. Keep on talking about yourself.
2. If you're asked something you don't know, pretend you do know!
3. Give the impression that you are superior to the person you are talking to.
4. Never talk about Jesus.
5. Allow yourself to be sidetracked by diversionary tactics.

HOW TO SHARE YOUR FAITH
Hot tip No 4:

Don't procrastinate because it is such tough work. Remember: you are helping to lead people to a righteous, sin-forgiven life.

"Those who are wise will shine like the brightness of the heavens, and those who lead many to righteousness, like the stars for ever and ever." *Daniel 12:3*

Five handy things to remember

1. Only *God* converts anyone.
2. Remember the things that helped you to become a Christian.
3. Ask someone else to pray for you before you share your faith.
4. Attend a course with other Christians on How to Share Your Faith.
5. Remember who Jesus is: that will help you to focus on him.

Softly, softly

Start where people are

Don't use the same approach with everyone you meet. Find out where people are in their spiritual understanding and start there. Some people are acutely aware of a sense of guilt, others are lonely, or feel that life is meaningless.

It's pointless spending countless hours covering the arguments for the existence of God with someone who has no problems over God's existence.

Q. Did Jesus have a purpose in telling the parables of the lost coin, the lost sheep and the lost son?

A. Definitely. Jesus had a special insight into the spiritual condition of everyone he met. But he used this insight to ensure that he applied an aspect of the gospel which was most appropriate for that person.

"Now the tax collectors and 'sinners' were all gathering around to hear him. But the Pharisees and the teachers of the law muttered, 'This man welcomes sinners and eats with them.' Then Jesus told them this parable."
Luke 15:1-3

The three famous parables of the lost coin, the lost sheep and the prodigal son were told against the background of the resentment that the top religious leaders had towards the way Jesus mixed with ordinary people.

Spiritual hints about sharing your faith

Pray
And what should you pray for?
a. Ask for the Holy Spirit to help you.
"So he said to me, 'This is the word of the Lord to Zerubbabel: Not by might, nor by power, but by my Spirit,' says the Lord Almighty." *Zechariah 4:6*

b. Ask for boldness.
"The wicked man flees though no one pursues, but the righteous are as bold as a lion." *Proverbs 28:1*
c. Be soul-conscious
Do you have a prayer list of people who are not Christians that you are regularly praying for?

Some practical hints

If you go visiting at a person's home, here are some practical hints.

1. Your dress. Don't draw attention to yourself.
2. Your breath. Take some breath mints with you.
3. Your cleanliness. Take a shower before you go!
4. Take a Bible or New Testament with you.
5. Go armed with literature you may wish to leave behind.
6. Go in twos. It is safer. You can pray together and encourage each other, and learn from each other. That's how Jesus sent out his disciples. "After this the Lord appointed seventy-two others and sent them *two by two* ahead of him to every town and place where he was about to go." *Luke 10:1*
7. When you are in somebody's home, you are a guest. Don't argue. Be pleasant and courteous.

I failed!

QUOTATION FROM A FAITHFUL SOUL WINNER TO SET YOU THINKING

"Christ sent me to preach the gospel and he will look after the results."
Mary Slessor

Success versus faithfulness
Jesus never said that everyone would respond in a positive way when they hear the gospel. So don't be discouraged when you spend a whole evening knocking on doors or an afternoon visiting a hospital ward and no one seems to be interested in Jesus. What matters is that we are faithful, not that we are successful.

And if you are successful ...
A word of warning. When the seventy-two disciples returned to Jesus they were full of joy and said, "Lord, even the demons submit to us in your name." But Jesus, rather surprisingly, replied, "Do not rejoice that the spirits submit to you, but rejoice that your names are written in heaven." *Luke 10:17, 20*

So we don't rejoice in our success, but rejoice in the fact that people are coming to know Jesus.

Jesus and the rich young man

"Now a man came up to Jesus and asked, 'Teacher, what good thing must I do to get eternal life?'

'Why do you ask me about what is good?' Jesus replied. 'There is only One who is good. If you want to enter life, obey the commandments.'

'Which ones?' the man inquired. Jesus replied, '"Do not murder, do not commit adultery, do not steal, do not give false testimony, honor your father and mother," and "love your neighbor as yourself."'

'All these I have kept,' the young man said. 'What do I still lack?' Jesus answered, 'If you want to be perfect, go, sell your possessions and give to the poor, and you will have treasure in heaven. Then come, follow me.'

When the young man heard this, he went away sad, because he had great wealth."

Matthew 19:16-22

What went wrong?

The rich young man did many things that we would say were right.

1. He went to the right person – Jesus. *Matthew 19:16*
2. He went in the right frame of mind – he "fell on his knees" before Jesus. *See Mark 10:17*
3. He asked the right question – how to find "eternal life." *Matthew 19:16*

But it all ended in tears! The young man is the only person in the Gospels who is recorded as having left Jesus "sad."

So did Jesus fail?

"The young man ... went away sad." That doesn't sound much like a success story.

Clearly, since Jesus was the Son of God, he did not do anything wrong here or anywhere else.

Visibly, the love of money gripped this young man's heart.

This young man was jolted into seeing the stark choice he had to make between following Jesus and following something else. All we can do is simply present this choice.

What about children?

Children and evangelism

Many people are more tongue-tied about introducing Jesus to children than they are to adults. Don't let anybody deceive you into feeling that children are too young to become followers of Jesus.

The example of Jesus

In Jesus' day, children not only had no rights, they were often so overlooked that they were made to feel that they hardly counted.

So Jesus' attitude to children was most remarkable.

Mark 10:13-16

Verse 13	"People were bringing little children to Jesus to have him touch them, but the disciples rebuked them.
Verse 14	When Jesus saw this, he was indignant. He said to them, 'Let the little children come to me, and do not hinder them, for the kingdom of God belongs to such as these.
Verse 15	I tell you the truth, anyone who will not receive the kingdom of God like a little child will never enter it.'
Verse 16	And he took the children in his arms, put his hands on them and blessed them."

Points to note

1. Ordinary people expected Jesus to help children in a spiritual way – *verse 13.*
2. The disciples wanted to brush the children to one side – *verse 13.*
3. Jesus was not indifferent to children but he was "indignant" toward those disciples with wrong attitudes – *verse 14.*
4. We have Jesus' specific command concerning child evangelism – "Let the little children come to me" – *verse 14.*
5. Jesus loved children and blessed them – *verse 16.*

The Wordless Book

You can make your own wordless book to use with children. Here is how it could be used.

"Hi! Have you ever seen a book with no words in it?

Here's my book which has no words. Watch out for the different colors. Each color tells a story.

Gold page

This gold page stands for heaven. The streets of heaven are made of pure gold.

Jesus has gone to heaven to prepare a place for each of his friends.

In heaven there will be no more crying, no more sadness and no more illness.

Dark page

The dark page is a sad page. It reminds us of our sin. It helps us remember anything that we have done or anything that we have said or anything that we have thought which did not please God.

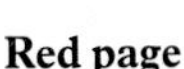

Red page

This red page is both a sad page and a happy page.

It is a sad page because it reminds us of Jesus dying on the cross.

It is a happy page because it reminds us that Jesus died so our sins can be forgiven.

White page

This clean page is your page in this story.

It stands for the moment we ask Jesus to be our special friend and accept him as our Savior.

Green cover

Did you notice the color of the cover of the book?

The green cover of my wordless book reminds me to grow. Jesus is happy if we desire to grow and be more like him.

These are the five colors of my wordless book. Each color has a secret story. See if you can remember what each one is."

There are so many oddballs and fanatics around

Who says who is an oddball ?

Is an oddball someone carrying a sandwich board proclaiming: "The end of the world is nigh"? Many would say that you are an oddball for reading a book like this.

Beware of judging other Christians and writing them off: "Do not judge, or you too will be judged" *Matthew 7:1.*

Some would say that anyone who engages in personal evangelism is a fanatic. Occasionally there will be people who are far from being mentally stable and who attach themselves to a Christian fellowship. Rather than being a reason for embarrassment – that should be a reason to rejoice that such people find help within a Christian group.

They don't belong to us/our church

Beware of rejecting the ministry and gospel proclamation of other Christians. Remember that Jesus said: "Whoever is not against us is for us."

> "'Teacher,' said John, 'we saw a man driving out demons in your name and we told him to stop, because he was not one of us.' 'Do not stop him,' Jesus said. 'No one who does a miracle in my name can in the next moment say anything bad about me, for whoever is not against us is for us. I tell you the truth, anyone who gives you a cup of water in my name because you belong to Christ will certainly not lose his reward.'" *Mark 9:38-41.*

HOW TO SHARE YOUR FAITH
Hot tip No 5:
Don't worry if you are labeled as an oddball.
Paul was pronounced insane by Festus. "Festus interrupted Paul's defense. 'You are out of your mind, Paul!' he exclaimed. 'Your great learning is driving you insane.'" *Acts 26:24.*

Witnessing for Jesus is a serious business

Read through Matthew 13:36-43		**Lessons to learn about witnessing**
Verse 36	Then he left the crowd and went into the house. His disciples came to him and said, "Explain to us the parable of the weeds in the field."	**1.** Seek wisdom from Jesus
Verse 37	He answered, "The one who sowed the good seed is the Son of Man."	**2.** We must work with Jesus **3.** We must believe that the Bible is good
Verse 38	"The field is the world, and the good seed stands for the sons of the kingdom. The weeds are the sons of the evil one,"	**4.** There is no limit to where we should witness
Verse 39	"and the enemy who sows them is the devil. The harvest is the end of the age, and the harvesters are angels."	**5.** We must never underestimate Satan's power **6.** We must remember that there will be a harvest
Verses 40-42	"As the weeds are pulled up and burned in the fire, so it will be at the end of the age. The Son of Man will send out his angels, and they will weed out of his kingdom everything that causes sin and all who do evil. They will throw them into the fiery furnace, where there will be weeping and gnashing of teeth."	**7.** We must remember what will happen to the wicked
Verse 43	"Then the righteous will shine like the sun in the kingdom of their Father. He who has ears, let him hear."	**8.** We must always be grateful for our salvation in Jesus

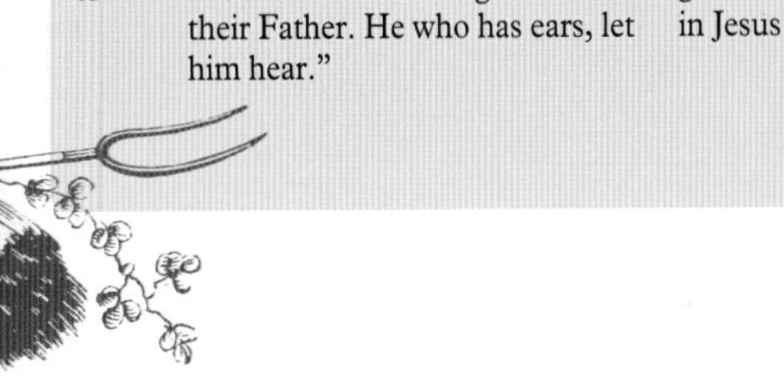

I'm no good at speaking

Excuses, excuses, excuses!

If we all waited until we thought that we were fully equipped to share our faith, no personal evangelism would ever take place.

"I'm not a good speaker," is a favorite excuse. But don't worry, if God wants you to be a good speaker either in public or on a one-to-one basis, *he* will equip you.

Remember Moses?

Read through Exodus 3:11–4:12.

- God was appointing Moses to lead his people out of Egypt. *Exodus 3:12*
- Moses' complaint – "I'm not a good speaker."
  "Moses said to the Lord, 'O Lord, I have never been eloquent, neither in the past nor since you have spoken to your servant. I am slow of speech and of tongue.'" *Exodus 4:10*
- The Lord's reply – "I will teach you."
  "The Lord said to him [Moses], 'Who gave man his mouth? Who makes him deaf or mute? Who gives him sight or makes him blind? Is it not I, the Lord? Now go; I will help you speak and will teach you what to say.'" *Exodus 4:11-12*

Remember Paul?

Paul was a theological elitist. He went to the best Bible college of his day. He was one of the leading theologians among the Jews, and became perhaps the greatest Christian thinker, theologian and missionary strategist of all time.

But he was conscious of his *weakness*! He knew that sharing Jesus was always a spiritual battle. So he always remained fully aware of his own human weakness but relied totally on God's spiritual power.

> "When I am *weak*, then I am strong."
> *2 Corinthians 12:10*

> "I can do everything through him [Jesus] who gives me strength."
> *Philippians 4:13*

The Roman road to salvation

Here's how the outline of the gospel can be simply explained from Paul's wonderful letter to the Romans.

1. A sinner has a problem – the sin problem

a. Romans says we have all sinned.

"There is no one righteous, not even one." *Romans 3:10 See also Romans 3:23*

b. Romans says that spiritual death is the result of unforgiven sin.

"For the wages of sin is death, but the gift of God is eternal life in Christ Jesus our Lord." *Romans 6:23*

2. The solution to the sin problem

Romans says God has provided the way out for sinners.

"But God demonstrates his own love for us in this: While we were still sinners, Christ died for us." *Romans 5:8. See also Romans 5:12; Romans 2:4*

3. The action a sinner must take

a. Romans says a sinner must accept Jesus as Savior.

"That if you confess with your mouth; 'Jesus is Lord,' and believe in your heart that God raised him from the dead, you will be saved." *Romans 10:9*

b. Romans says that new believers then re-enact the death, burial and resurrection through baptism.

"Or don't you know that all of us who were baptized into Christ Jesus were baptized into his death? We were therefore buried with him through baptism to death in order that, just as Christ was raised from the dead ... we too may live a new life." *Romans 6:3-4*

Opportunity knocks

Learning how to do it

One of the best ways to learn about sharing our faith in Jesus with others is to see how the first followers of Jesus did this.

Read through Acts 8:26-40 to see what it teaches you about leading a person to Jesus.

Acts 8:26-40

26 Now an angel of the Lord said to Philip, "Go south to the road – the desert road – that goes down from Jerusalem to Gaza."	Philip was open to God's leading. Philip had just been involved in preaching the gospel to crowds of people in a city. Now he obeyed the Lord and went off to the desert. *See Acts 8:4-7.*
27 So he started out, and on his way he met an Ethiopian eunuch, an important official in charge of all the treasury of Candace, queen of the Ethiopians. This man had gone to Jerusalem to worship,	Wealth and an important job did not satisfy the spiritual longing of this government official.
28 and on his way home was sitting in his chariot reading the book of Isaiah the prophet.	The Bible is the best book to use in sharing your faith. This man was already reading it!
29 The Spirit told Philip, "Go to that chariot and stay near it."	Philip was alert to the Spirit. Philip obeyed even if he may not have known why he had to run alongside this chariot.
30 Then Philip ran up to the chariot and heard the man reading Isaiah the prophet. "Do you understand what you are reading?" Philip asked.	Philip did not beat about the bush. He asked a question. He wanted to find out what spiritual understanding the Ethiopian had.
31 "How can I," he said, "unless someone explains it to me?" So he invited Philip to come up and sit with him.	Philip used this God-given opportunity and jumped up into the chariot. You can lead a person to Jesus, no matter where you are.

32 The eunuch was reading this passage of Scripture: "He was led like a sheep to the slaughter, and as a lamb before the shearer is silent, so he did not open his mouth. *33* In his humiliation he was deprived of justice. Who can speak of his descendants? For his life was taken from the earth." *34* The eunuch asked Philip, "Tell me, please, who is the prophet talking about, himself or someone else?"	The Ethiopian was in a bit of a quandary, for he clearly did not understand what he was reading. But he wanted someone to help him.
35 Then Philip began with that very passage of Scripture and told him the good news about Jesus.	Philip used the Bible to explain to him about the good news of Jesus.
36 As they traveled along the road, they came to some water and the eunuch said, "Look, here is water. Why shouldn't I be baptized?" *38* And he gave orders to stop the chariot. Then both Philip and the eunuch went down into the water and Philip baptized him.	The Ethiopian opened his heart to Jesus. *(Verse 37 is a footnote in many Bibles, because it only comes in late manuscripts. It is a wonderful testimony of faith in Jesus. "Philip said, 'If you believe with all your heart, you may.' The eunuch answered, 'I believe that Jesus Christ is the Son of God.'")* Philip baptized the Ethiopian there and then. Baptism was the first response after he accepted Christ.
39 When they came up out of the water, the Spirit of the Lord suddenly took Philip away, and the eunuch did not see him again, but went on his way rejoicing.	Philip continued to be open to the Spirit of the Lord. Somebody else would have to provide follow-up for the new Ethiopian Christian. The Ethiopian rejoiced in Jesus.
40 Philip, however, appeared at Azotus and traveled about, preaching the gospel in all the towns until he reached Caesarea.	Philip carried on being faithful in serving Jesus.

A golden verse

Acts 8:35 is one of the most helpful verses in the Bible about how to lead a person to Jesus. Memorize it. Ask God to help you to follow it when you share your faith.

Don't ever forget the Holy Spirit

QUOTATION FROM A FAITHFUL SOUL WINNER TO SET YOU THINKING

"There is no better evangelist in the world than the Holy Spirit."
D.L. Moody

Who gives spiritual life?

Answer: Only the Holy Spirit. Work done trusting in human efforts gives no spiritual life. Work done trusting in the Holy Spirit is work done for eternity.

Jesus stated this key principle: "Flesh gives birth to flesh, but the Spirit gives birth to spirit." *John 3:6.*

The work of the Holy Spirit in John's gospel

What the Holy Spirit does	Quotation	Bible reference
1. He gives spiritual life	"The Spirit gives life."	*John 6:63*
2. He lives inside believers	"He lives with you and will be in you."	*John 14:17; Romans 8:9*
3. He witnesses to Jesus	"He will testify about me."	*John 15:26*
4. He honors and praises Jesus	"He will bring glory to me."	*John 16:14*
5. He convicts people about sin	"When he comes, he will convict the world of guilt in regard to sin and righteousness and judgment: in regard to sin, because men do not believe in me; in regard to righteousness, because I am going to the Father, where you can see me no longer; and in regard to judgment, because the prince of this world now stands condemned."	*John 16:8-11*
6. He convicts people about righteousness		*John 16:8-11*
7. He convicts people about judgment		*John 16:8-11*

No preparation needed?

There is one kind of occasion when Jesus said we should not try to work out in advance how to witness for him.

It is during any kind of persecution. Then, "you will be given what to say."

> "Be on your guard against men; they will hand you over to the local councils and flog you in their synagogues. On my account you will be brought before governors and kings as witnesses to them and to the Gentiles. But when they arrest you, do not worry about what to say or how to say it. At that time you will be given what to say, for it will not be you speaking, but the Spirit of your Father speaking through you." *Matthew 10:17-20.*

Of course this means that we should never be surprised when persecution comes our way. We are never left on our own to witness as the Holy Spirit promises to be with us all the time.

A word of warning

Don't expect too much too soon from a new Christian. Different people grow and develop at different rates, both physically and spiritually.

Don't give a new Christian the impression that he has to keep a whole list of new rules such as:

1. Do this …
2. Do this …
3. Do this …
4. Don't do this …
5. Don't do this …
6. Don't do this …

There's really only one important thing: *to develop his/her friendship with Jesus.*

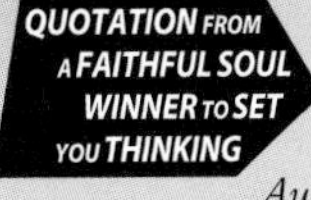

"One loving soul sets another on fire."
Augustine of Hippo.

The power of a Christ-like life

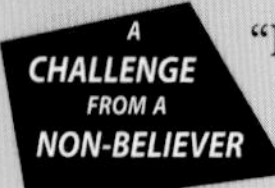

"His disciples have to look more saved if I am to believe in the Savior."
Nietzche

Where was the name "Christian" first used?

It first occurs in the Acts of the Apostles. Barnabas and Paul met with and taught the Christians in this place for a year.

> Then, "the disciples were called Christians first at Antioch."
> *Acts 11:26*

They turned the world upside down for Jesus

While Christians rejoiced over the "the spread of the gospel," non-Christians referred to this evangelism as "trouble".

> "These men who have caused trouble all over the world have now come here." *Acts 17:6*

Divine power

Luke's record in the Acts of the Apostles shows how Christians turned the world upside down.

They were the first to say that it was only through the power of Jesus in their lives.

The following verses describe what happened to Peter and John after they had been illegally locked in prison for the night.

They knew that they had been with Jesus

1. It was quite a gathering

2. Where do Christians find their power?

3. They kept on being filled with the Holy Spirit

4. They kept Jesus at the center of their witness

5. They always linked Jesus and salvation

6. Others saw that they had been with the risen Jesus

Letting the light of Jesus shine
Jesus once said: "Let your light shine before men, that they may see your good deeds and praise your Father in heaven." *Matthew 5:16*

HOW TO SHARE YOUR FAITH
Hot tip No 6:
Your life can be as much a witness for Jesus as anything you ever say.
"Religion is caught, not taught."
Dean W.R. Inge

Jesus was dead and buried, but his followers still knew him as he was alive in the Spirit.

"The next day the rulers, elders and teachers of the law met in Jerusalem. Annas the high priest was there, and so were Caiaphas, John, Alexander and the other men of the high priest's family."	*Acts 4:5-6*
"They had Peter and John brought before them and began to question them: 'By what power or what name did you do this?'"	*Acts 4:7*
"Then Peter, filled with the Holy Spirit, said to them: 'Rulers and elders of the people! If we are being called to account today for an act of kindness shown to a cripple and are asked how he was healed, then know this, you and all the people of Israel:'"	*Acts 4:8-10*
"It is by the name of Jesus Christ of Nazareth, whom you crucified but whom God raised from the dead, that this man stands before you healed. He is '"the stone you builders rejected, which has become the capstone."'	*Acts 4:10-11*
"Salvation is found in no one else, for there is no other name under heaven given to men by which we must be saved."	*Acts 4:12*
"When they saw the courage of Peter and John and realized that they were unschooled, ordinary men, they were astonished and they took note that *these men had been with Jesus.*"	*Acts 4:13*

The importance of preaching

QUOTATION FROM A FAITHFUL SOUL WINNER TO SET YOU THINKING

"Millions have never heard the name of Jesus. Hundreds of millions have seen a missionary only once in their lives, and know nothing of our King. Shall we let them perish? Can we go to our beds and sleep while China, India, Japan, and other nations are being damned? Are we clear of their blood? Have they no claim upon us? We ought to put it on this footing –
not 'Can I prove that I *ought* to go?'
but 'Can I prove that I *ought not* to go?'
C.H. Spurgeon

One-on-one witnessing and preaching

You could adapt the above quote and say, "Millions have never had the way of salvation explained to them on a one-on-one basis."

The priority of preaching

Preaching about the Lord is extremely important in most churches and denominations, but for some churches it is out of style and not fashionable.

The apostle Paul was clear about its permanent importance.

> "'Everyone who calls on the name of the Lord will be saved.' How, then, can they call on the one they have not believed in? And how can they believe in the one of whom they have not heard? And how can they hear without someone *preaching* to them? And how can they preach unless they are sent? As it is written, 'How beautiful are the feet of those who bring good news.'" *Romans 10:13-15*

There will never be an overabundance of Christian preachers in God's church.

Making use of sermons

- Invite someone to an evangelistic service or special preaching meeting.
- Lend a cassette of a good gospel sermon to a friend.

A ten point charter for Christian witnessing

1.	Why we do it	*Romans 1:14*
2.	Our special prayer	*Matthew 9:38*
3.	Our special helper	*Philippians 4:13*
4.	Our point of focus	*John 3:16*
5.	Our reward	*1 Thessalonains 2:19-20*
6.	Our power	"But you will receive power when the Holy Spirit comes on you; and you will be my witnesses in Jerusalem, and in all Judea and Samaria, and to the ends of the earth." *Acts 1:8*
7.	Our message	*Romans 1:16*
8.	Our cutting edge	*2 Timothy 4:2*
9.	Our moment to speak	*2 Corinthians 6:2*
10.	A great example	*Mark 5:19-20*

You are unique

A QUOTATION TO SET YOU THINKING

"The gospel does not fall from the clouds like rain by accident, but is brought by the hands of men and women to whom God has sent it."
John Calvin

Some sobering facts

- You may be the only Christian some of your family and friends know.
- Many religious people and, probably, many of your co-workers and friends have never had the actual good news of Jesus presented to them.

Where should I begin?

Start where you are!

> "As Jesus was getting into the boat, the man who had been demon-possessed begged to go with him. Jesus did not let him, but said, 'Go home to your family and tell them how much the Lord has done for you, and how he has had mercy on you.'" *Mark 5:18-19*

Many people find that their families are the hardest people to witness to. But Jesus told this new disciple that that was where he had to start.

"But I'm not as gifted as many other people"

Don't worry about how many gifts and talents you have. Put to work the ones you do have.

Read the parable of the talents from *Matthew 25:14-30.*

Note that the three people in the story were given a *different number of talents*. In the parable, the person who used his five talents and the person who used his two talents were commended with the same words:

> "'Well done, good and faithful servant! You have been faithful with a few things; I will put you in charge of many things.'"
> *Matthew 25:21 and 23*

In the parable the person who was condemned was the one who had been given one talent. Why? Because he did not bother to use it. He just hid it in the ground.

Chosen by God

To complain about our lack of gifts is to come close to insulting our Creator. Think about what you do possess:

a. You were chosen by God before the world was created.

"For he chose us in him before the creation of the world." *Ephesians 1:4*

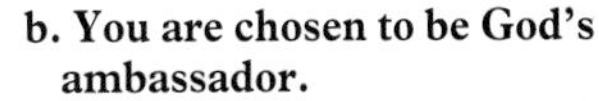

b. You are chosen to be God's ambassador.

"We are therefore Christ's *ambassadors*, as though God were making his appeal through us. We implore on Christ's behalf: Be reconciled to God." *2 Corinthians 5:20*

c. It is Jesus' wish that you should be fruitful.

"I am the vine; you are the branches. If a man remains in me and I in him, he will bear much fruit; apart from me you can do nothing." *John 15:5*

Stardom versus obscurity

There is a tendency in some Christian circles to place on a pedestal the famous people who have become Christians, especially if they are famous sports personalities or well-known entertainers.

How different that is from the early days of Christianity. Here Paul is writing to encourage the Christians at Corinth to remember who they were in the eyes of the world when God called them into his kingdom.

> "Brothers, think of what you were when you were called. Not many of you were wise by human standards; not many were influential; not many were of noble birth. But God chose the foolish things of the world to shame the wise; God chose the weak things of the world to shame the strong. He chose the lowly things of this world and the despised things – and the things that are not – to nullify the things that are, so that no one may boast before him." *1 Corinthians 1:26-29*

Using the Internet

What's the point in using the Internet?

1. The person you are trying to help can follow the steps to faith in Jesus at his/her own speed.
2. He/she can do this when it is most convenient to him/her.
3. This can be done in privacy.
4. The best evangelistic sites on the Internet are easy to follow.
5. These Internet sites have been compiled by dedicated Christian evangelists and evangelistic organizations. Their teaching is probably clearer than anything most other Christians can manage.

How is the Internet used in personal evangelism?

Just give a list of the following sites to your friend or e-mail them to him/her.

http://www.grahamassn.org/bgea/bgeasal/bgeastps.htm
This site and the other three mentioned on this page were set up by the Billy Graham Evangelistic Association.

This one introduces a person to Jesus. It is called *Steps to peace with God.*

http://www.grahamassn.org/bgea/bgeasal/follow.htm
This site is ideal for a brand new Christian. It even has a follow up letter from Billy Graham.

http://www.grahamassn.org/bgea/bgeasal/salmain.htm
This site contains answers to some of the most frequently asked questions about the Christian faith.

http://www.gospelcom.net
This site lists over one hundred Christian organizations that can provide help and assistance in growing as a Christian.